for
beginners

Abstract Game Design for Beginners

Design Games That Focus on Pure Strategy and Logic, Often with Minimal Thematic Elements

Printed in the United States of America

First Edition: 2025

This copyright page includes the necessary copyright notice, permissions request information, acknowledgments for the cover design, interior design, and editing, as well as the details of the first edition.

www.littlebiggiant.com

Introduction

A laptop glowed on the kitchen table. A young player watched a recorded match. The board was simple. Black and white stones. No story. No plastic soldiers. Just choices. In March 2016, a program called AlphaGo beat Lee Sedol four games to one. That fact flashed on the screen. It felt strange. The game did not need a castle or a spaceship to be fierce. It only needed rules. It only needed thinking. A short, bright move on the screen made the player lean closer. "How did it see that?" slipped out. The question sounded small and a little scared. The room felt quiet and urgent. Abstract games work like that. They test pure strategy and logic. They often have very little theme. That is what Abstract

Game Design for Beginners teaches: Design Games That Focus on Pure Strategy and Logic, Often with Minimal Thematic Elements. The line of proof is simple and real. Computers and champions can reach deep ideas from tiny rules. A single rule change can flip the whole board.

Hands hovered over a small stack of pieces. Paper and a pencil waited. The choice was clear and terrifying. Start with one rule, then test it. Change one thing, then test again. That is the step from watching a famous match to making something new. It sounds doable and it sounds hard. Which rule will be tried first? Which mistake will become the idea that matters? The next move could be a failure. Or it could be the first spark of a game that teaches thinking like a champion. Which will it be?

Table of Contents

Chapter 1

Principles of Abstract Game Design

By the end of this chapter you will be able to define abstraction in your own game designs and describe how to balance clarity, depth, and elegance.

Defining abstraction: stripping theme to mechanics

Step 1. Identify the essential actions. You start by listing every move a player makes in your game. Then ask: which actions are truly necessary for play, and which are merely decorative? The goal is to keep only the moves, placements, and consequences that shape the core decisions players face. When you strip away theme, you should still be able to answer: what can a player do on their turn, and what happens as a result? The result is a clean set of mechanics that can travel across different skins or stories without breaking.

Step 2. Separate mechanics from story. Theme is the clothes; mechanics are the bones. Remove any narrative excuses for why something exists and focus on why a rule exists at all. For example, if your game involves a knight collecting gems in a dungeon, ask: could the same core actions—placing a marker, moving to an adjacent space, and capturing a neighbor—work on a plain grid without dragons or dungeons? If yes, you have a candidate abstraction. If not, rephrase the action so that its effect, not its tale, remains.

Step 3. Test minimal boards and actions. Build a tiny version of your idea with a few pieces and a small board. Let two players play a handful of turns to reveal which choices matter. The aim is clarity: can you see, from the first few moves, which decisions push toward victory? If you notice that some rules never affect outcomes, trim them. If certain moves repeatedly confuse players, simplify them. Two quick micro-cases help you see the value of abstraction in action:

Micro-case A: Territory-style simplification. Imagine you start with a square grid and a single kind of marker. The goal is to enclose space, not to conquer a thematic realm. Players place markers one by one; surrounding an empty area earns points, but you don't score for fancy rituals—only for controlled space. After a few turns, you notice that the core tension is about balance between expansion and closing gaps. The surrounding rule itself is the mechanic; the story is irrelevant. The takeaway is that ambition and strategy live in the mechanic, not in the narrative.

Micro-case B: Direct-conflict simplification. Take a thematic chase game and strip it to two types of moves: place a piece and capture an adjacent opponent piece by surrounding it. On a 3x3 or 4x4 board, players see two kinds of choices that matter: where to place to threaten the opponent, and where to defend. The drama comes from interaction, not from the fantasy. If players can quickly learn to create forks or traps, you've distilled the tension into simple, repeatable dynamics.

Step 4. Decide what stays and what goes. After playing these pared-down versions, ask: which rules are essential to the decisions players make? If a rule doesn't influence who wins or what patterns emerge, drop it. If you keep a rule but it never changes outcomes, consider making it optional or turning it into a teachable example rather than a constant requirement. Abstraction is not the removal of complexity; it is the removal of unnecessary complexity so that the meaningful decisions stand out.

Step 5. Preserve transferability. A strong abstraction should be easy to port to different sizes, numbers of pieces, or even different themes while preserving its core tension. If you can swap the board for a larger grid, or replace markers with tokens of a different color, and the game still behaves like the same idea, you've achieved portability. Portability helps you test and balance more quickly, and it makes your design adaptable for future creativity.

Step 6. Capture the essence in a rules draft. Write a concise set of rules that focuses on the three questions: What can you do? What happens when you do it? How do you win? A crisp rule set makes it easier for new players to learn, quick playtests to reveal edge cases, and designers to refine without dragging in irrelevant components. The essence here is that good rules translate action into consequence with no extraneous decoration.

Core design goals: clarity, depth, elegance

Step 1. Clarity first: rules that can be taught fast and executed without confusion. Clarity means that a beginner can read the rules once and play a few turns with minimal guidance. Use precise terms, avoid conflicting terms, and test the rules with players who have not seen the game before. If someone misinterprets a rule, you have found a source of ambiguity you must fix. Clarity is the foundation that makes depth and elegance possible.

Step 2. Depth through meaningful decisions: depth isn't sheer length or more rules. It's the long line of decisions that reveals new possibilities as the game progresses. Each turn should offer choices that matter in future moves, not repeats of the same safe option. Depth grows when strategies interact over time, creating tension between short-term gains and long-term plans. You don't need many rules to achieve depth; you need the right structure that makes consequences multi-step and consequential.

Step 3. Elegance as a practical virtue: elegance is about minimalism that yields rich play. Elegant games feel inevitable in retrospect: every rule makes sense, and every move you think of fits naturally into the emerging patterns. Too many exceptions or special cases break elegance and slow learning. Strive for a small, coherent set of rules that unlocks surprising, sometimes elegant, outcomes. You know you're close when players begin to discuss why a certain sequence is brilliant, not why a rule exists.

Step 4. Teachability as a tool for balance: if your game is easy to teach but quickly becomes shallow, you need a tweak, not more rules. If it's hard to teach but surprisingly deep, you may be on the right track but need clearer examples and a better progression. A teaching path—guided introductions that reveal core mechanics first, then layered complexity—helps players feel mastery without drowning in jargon.

Step 5. Balance with symmetry and tempo: symmetry, where each side has equal opportunities, is a powerful concept for clarity and fairness. Tempo, the pace of play, matters for depth. A game should reward good timing and thoughtful planning rather than lucky breaks. When you test, watch for moments where one choice consistently dominates; if that happens, you have a suffocating design, not a balanced one. You want a rhythm where both players feel they can influence the board meaningfully.

Step 6. Consistency across scales: test whether a design behaves similarly on small boards and larger boards. If a rule only works on a big board, or a move loses its meaning on a tiny board, you're trading elegance for scale-specific quirks. A consistent mechanic scales gracefully, helping both clarity and depth.

Player interaction models: direct conflict, territory, resource-less systems

Step 1. Direct conflict: players aim to capture or remove the opponent's pieces. The tension comes from direct opposition and immediate threats. In these models, visibility of moves and responses matters a lot; a single strong threat can shift the entire board. The logic of direct conflict favors sharp calculation and quick pattern recognition. An easy test: can you create a forced sequence where one bad move loses material or position? If yes, you've captured the essence of direct conflict.

Step 2. Territory: players seek to control space on the board, often without needing to eliminate the opponent's pieces outright. The reward is long-term influence, and the scoring emerges from controlled areas. The mental pull of territory is about balance: expanding enough to claim value while not overextending and opening lines for the opponent. This model rewards strategic planning, thread through sequences, and the ability to foresee how local moves influence global control. A tiny micro-case on a 3x3 or 4x4 board can illustrate how early choices shape late-game dominance.

Step 3. Resource-less systems: no resource pools, currencies, or countdowns to manage. The pressure comes from the arrangement of pieces and possible moves rather than resource management. You focus on spatial relationships, move legality, and long-range consequences. The speed of the game depends on how quickly meaningful options appear and how effectively players convert opportunities into advantage. A good resource-less example shows that even with simple moves, players can create intricate positional dynamics that require careful attention and patience.

Step 4. Choosing a primary model for your design. Start with one dominant interaction model and build the rest of the game around it. If you begin with direct conflict, you'll shape rules toward capture opportunities and defensive responses. If territory is your compass, you'll design scoring, local control, and life-or-death decisions about shape and influence. If resource-less play suits you, you'll focus on spatial balance, move legality, and the feel of elegant restriction. You can later blend models, but a clear primary model gives your design coherence and a path for learning the game.

Step 5. Examples in practice. Consider two mini sketches that illustrate these models without extra fluff.

Example 1: Direct conflict in a small grid. On a 4x4 board, players place one marker per turn with the goal of capturing an adjacent enemy marker by surrounding it on three sides. The core choices are where to threaten and where to defend. The simplest wins emerge from a few turning points where a single move changes which captures are possible in the next turn. This shows how direct conflict creates immediate pressure and sharp response.

Example 2: Territory on a modest board. On a 5x5 grid, players place markers to enclose empty spaces. Scoring favors larger controlled areas but avoids letting a single move secure a big chunk too easily. The tension comes from balancing expansion with the risk of giving the opponent access to larger pockets of space. The lesson is that territory-based play rewards long-range planning and careful zoning of the board, not just nimble tactics.

Two short micro-cases in action

Micro-case C: Territory pressure on a 3x3 board. Player A expands one line to press into the corner; Player B responds by contesting a cross-point that could unlock a bigger area. A few moves later, both players adjust to the growing frontier, and a decision about retreat or advance becomes pivotal. You see how small boards crystallize the idea of controlling space through careful placement.

Micro-case D: Direct-threat snap. On a 4x4 board, Player A creates a fork of threats that forces

Player B to defend in two directions at once. If Player B misreads the timing, a single reply creates a winning line for Player A. This demonstrates how direct conflict can create dramatic moments and teach players to anticipate responses.

Exercises

1) Quick abstraction drill (10 minutes). Take a familiar game you enjoy and rewrite its rules to strip theme away. Write a one-paragraph summary of the new mechanics, plus a one-sentence win condition. Play a quick round with a friend to test whether the mechanics are clear and whether the win condition feels satisfying. Record what surprised you and what felt too easy or too hard.

2) Balance check (15 minutes). Create a tiny prototype on graph paper: a small board, a couple of pieces per side, and a simple capture or scoring rule. Play three rounds. After each round, ask the players what move felt decisive and which rules were least understood. Adjust the rule slightly to remove confusion and note whether the balance improved.

3) Interaction focus (20 minutes). Choose one interaction model (direct conflict, territory, or resource-less) and design a 4x4 or 5x5 variant that emphasizes that model. Write down the top three decisions a player must consider each turn. Then play the variant twice and compare experiences: did

the model feel natural, and did the decisions feel meaningful and varied?

Troubleshooting: common problems and quick fixes

- Problem: Rules are hard to understand after the first read. Quick fix: rewrite them in the simplest present tense; add one short example rule in action per page; test with a new player who has no prior exposure.

- Problem: One move dominates play, making the game uninteresting. Quick fix: adjust the win condition or add a constraint that prevents looping or repetitive captures; consider a small rule change that introduces a second kind of consequence.

- Problem: The board feels empty; players have too few meaningful choices. Quick fix: introduce a second dimension of interaction, such as a capture mechanic, a scoring mechanic, or a tempo twist that makes every move carry future consequences.

- Problem: The game is too long for beginner playtests. Quick fix: cap the number of turns in early versions; ensure a clear, short path to victory or reset the state after a fixed number of moves so players can learn quickly.

Tools and templates

- Rule clarity checklist: (1) Is every term defined? (2) Are all actions described in the same tense? (3) Is there a single, unambiguous win condition? (4) Are edge cases described or solvable by a simple rule? (5) Can you teach the game in five minutes? Use this checklist after drafting rules and again after your first playtest.

- Quick balance sketch: draw a tiny board, list piece counts for each side, note the win condition, and record one or two balance metrics (symmetry, first-move advantage, tempo). Revisit after each round of playtesting.

- Playtest log template: date, players, board size, variant name, key decisions, outcomes, unexpected moves, suggested changes, next steps. Keeping a short log helps you notice patterns over time.

Key Takeaway: Abstraction is about keeping the moves that matter, so players can learn the rules quickly, learn the strategy faster, and enjoy the elegant ways simple decisions interact.

Transition: In the next chapter, we unpack History and Inspirations, looking at classic abstract games and what they teach, plus the math that underpins strategy. You'll see how Go, Chess, Mancala, Hex, and Othello illuminate the kinds of ideas that work well in abstract design, and you'll begin to map those ideas onto your own evolving toolkit. Coming up next: History and Inspirations.

Chapter 2

History and Inspirations

By the end of this chapter, you will see how classic abstract games teach simple rules that unlock deep strategy, understand the math behind why some positions win, and spot how designers turn ideas into new kinds of play.

Classic abstract games and what they teach

Go

Go starts with a grid and a single rule: place a stone on an empty point. From that simple idea grows a web of choices about where to build influence, where to protect it, and where to invade an opponent's space. The game rewards patience. You learn to read distant lines of play, not just the next move, because one stone can affect hours of future decisions. In Go, tactics and strategy blend: local fights may flare into global fights as groups connect, separate, or strand each other. This teaches designers how a tiny rule set can generate vast depth when players pursue long-term plans. A small-board example helps: on a five-by-five board, the first player often starts in a corner to seed influence, while the second player tries to extend toward the center to balance space. The result is a delicate dance between securing territory and keeping lines flexible for future moves.

Chess

Chess starts with 16 pieces per side and a clear goal: checkmate the opponent's king. Yet the rhythm of the game comes from development, positional pressure, and the tension between attack and defense. You learn to balance material with activity, to look several moves ahead, and to recognize patterns that recur across openings and endgames. For designers, Chess is a master class in turning a compact move set into a theatre of long-term planning. A simple two-move sequence—develop a knight, then bring a bishop to an active diagonal—illustrates the tempo and initiative that can decide a game long before the board is crowded. This teaches designers how early choices shape both opportunities and vulnerabilities later, a key idea when you're shaping rules that stay clean while offering room to surprise.

Mancala

Mancala games revolve around seed-like counters in pits, with moves that redistribute resources across your side and your opponent's. The core lessons are counting, timing, and control of momentum. Small decisions matter because each sow can create multiple future consequences: you may open a path to capture, you may starve your opponent, or you may set yourself up for a sweeping endgame. Mancala demonstrates how efficient rules can enable intricate planning, even without hidden information or complex pieces. For designers, the takeaway is how a modest board and a handful of moves can yield strategic richness through careful sequencing and foresight.

Hex

Hex is played on a hexagonal grid with two sides assigned to each player. The goal is to connect opposite sides with a continuous chain of your pieces. The rules are almost scary in their simplicity: no draws, ever; every move pushes you toward or away from a goal, often in ways you can't predict until several turns later. Hex teaches the power of connectivity and forcing moves. It shows how constraining geometry can force players into pathways they might not choose at first glance, which is a fundamental design insight: you can guide decision-making through the shape of the board itself. A micro-case might look like this: the first player places a stone to start a potential bridge, the second player blocks, and suddenly the board reveals a tension line that both players begin to follow, revealing the connected-sides dynamic.

Othello (Reversi)

Othello begins with a simple flipping mechanic: place a disk and flip any of your opponent's disks that are sandwiched between your new disk and another disk of yours. The result is a game of timing, parity, and edge control. Early moves open or close vast corridors of potential flips, and a single well-timed move can swing the whole board. This teaches designers about how a tiny, visible mechanic—turning discs—can create a cascade of strategic possibilities as boards fill and futures become constrained. A compact example on a small board shows how chasing stability near the corners can restrict your opponent's options, while overextending can invite a rapid swing in the opposite direction.

Mathematical foundations: combinatorial game theory basics

Abstract games shine when you separate the idea of “rules” from “moves.” In games with perfect information and no hidden randomness, you can study positions by asking who can force a win from a given setup. A central idea is that positions can be classified as winning for the next player to move (N-positions) or losing for the next player (P-positions). In a simple take-away game where a player may remove 1 or 2 tokens from a single pile, leaving a multiple of 3 to your opponent often creates a winning rhythm. If you can keep the opponent on positions that lead to a loss after every move, you stay on a path to victory. This is how many classic games convey the habit of looking ahead and planning a path rather than just reacting to each move.

Another useful idea is the sum of independent games. If you have two smaller games you can play in parallel, the best move isn't always in the first game you touch. Instead, you think about how moving in one game changes the balance of the other. This thinking is the seed of more advanced ideas, like Grundy numbers, which give a compact way to value a position by listing all possible moves and their consequences. For younger readers, the point to grasp is simple: some positions give you a clear path to victory, while others require you to balance several possible futures at once.

Theories of balance also show up in these studies. Designers use symmetry, predictable good patterns, and carefully limited options to shape how a game unfolds. If a game offers too many strong initial moves, it can become trivial; if it offers too few, it becomes dull. The middle ground—enough choices to feel meaningful but not so many that players flounder—often yields the most interesting play. In practice, you can test this by watching how new players explore a game: do they feel clever after a few turns, or do they wander, unsure of how to progress? The math behind these questions helps designers tune rules so fresh players can learn quickly while veterans still have meaningful decisions.

Notable designers and modern reinterpretations

Classic abstract games have long histories, but modern designers remix these ideas in new shapes and with newer audiences. In Hex, the idea of connecting opposite sides was realized independently by Piet Hein and John Nash, and it remains a touchstone for formal design thinking about connectivity and forcing moves. Othello was created by Goro Hasegawa in the 1970s and popularized through a broad appeal that emphasizes flipping dynamics and strategic tempo. Mancala, in its many regional variations, is ancient in origin and continues to inspire simple yet deep plays across different cultures, reminding designers that accessibility often fuels depth.

In recent decades, several designers have produced strong reinterpretations of abstract ideas:

- Tak, designed by James Ernest and Patrick Rothfuss, turns abstract strategy into a compact, highly tactile race for connection on a board with flat stones and walls. The game showcases how a modern pairing of a writer and a game designer can yield a brisk, elegant set of decisions that rewards foresight.

- Hive, by John Yianni, uses insect-shaped pieces on a seamless board with no fixed grid. Moves hinge on piece abilities and how they interact, producing emergent behavior that often surprises players who expect a familiar grid-based feel. This shows how changing the geometry and piece abilities can reframe what "space control" means.

- Quarto, designed by Blaise Müller, places 16 pieces with four binary traits on a four-by-four board. The catch is you choose the piece for your opponent to place, so you constantly adapt to what your opponent is steering you toward. Quarto demonstrates how information presentation and controlled choice can create tension and clever misdirection without changing the core move rule.

- The modern wave of abstract and hybrid games often blends these ideas with themes or tactile components, yet many still honor the core truth: simple rules can seed complex, satisfying play. Designers keep testing what happens when you tweak a single mechanic—how you place a piece, how options are revealed, or how a win condition is defined—and the entire design shifts. This ongoing experimentation helps players see how structure shapes strategy, a core lesson any beginner can apply when designing or analyzing games.

Key Takeaway: Simple rules can unlock deep, surprising strategy, and modern designers keep finding fresh ways to reveal that depth by reimagining how movement, visibility, and goals work together.

Coming up next Subtittle: Mechanics that Produce Strategy

1) Turn structure and move freedom,

2) Information visibility: perfect vs hidden information effects,

3) Determinism and randomness: balancing predictability and surprise.

Chapter 3

Mechanics that Produce Strategy

You feel the rhythm of a game first when you notice how many actions you get on your turn and how you're allowed to use them. Turn structure is the heartbeat of abstract design: it decides how fast or slow the game moves, how deeply you think between moves, and how many choices you have to weigh in a single moment. A straightforward game might give you one clear move per turn. That makes every choice crisp and duties of strategy tight. You can see threats, plan a few steps ahead, and feel a sense of momentum as you press your advantage. It's fast, focused, and easy to learn.

When you open the turn up, when you give players more freedom within a turn, you invite deeper thinking. You might allow several moves, or a mix of actions in one turn, or a turn with optional tweaks that can alter how the board looks next. This adds layers for you and your opponent, because every decision now carries more possible follow-ups. The game becomes less about guessing a single line of attack and more about managing a web of possibilities. The trick is to keep the number of good options from exploding. If every turn feels like wandering through a library with every door open, you might lose focus. If there are only two doors, strategy stays tidy but you risk boredom.

Two practical micro-cases help you feel the idea in action. Case A is a small grid game where each player places a single marker on their turn, trying to line up a pattern or block the other player. The choices feel meaningful because every placement changes which spots are safe, which threats remain, and which patterns are still possible. The pace stays quick, but you still feel the weight of your decision as you imagine how your opponent will respond next. Case B gives you a slightly richer field: on your turn you can either place a marker or perform a second action, like rotating a piece or swapping a marker's color. Now you juggle two kinds of moves, and you must decide whether to tighten your immediate threat or set up a longer plan. The balance between speed and depth shifts, and your brain learns to compare not just where to move, but when to move both ways.

If you're designing, ask yourself: How many moves should a turn contain? What counts as a "good" move in this system, and how many good moves exist in the typical moment of play? You can test by starting with one-move turns, then try adding a second action per turn in a controlled variant. Compare how the games feel: is it slower but more thoughtful, or does it stall because choices multiply too quickly? The aim is to give players enough freedom to feel clever, while keeping the game's goals clear and the path to victory visibly attainable.

From a teaching standpoint, you want a flow that rewards planning but doesn't punish a reasonable mistake. You want a level of predictability that lets players learn and improve, but with enough ambiguity that the best move isn't always obvious. Balancing turn structure means watching how players talk about their moves, how long they pause to decide, and how quickly they recover after a misstep. If players routinely stall for long periods, you may have too many viable options. If they finish turns in a blink and the game feels over too soon, you may need to dial back the freedom a notch.

Two quick reminders help when you're testing: keep the core objective front and center so every choice nudges toward that goal, and track how often players feel confident enough to take a risk versus play it safe. The more you test, the better you'll tune the sweet spot where freedom meets clarity. The result is a game that rewards clever planning without turning into a math marathon.

Information visibility: perfect vs hidden information effects

What players can see directly shapes what they can plan for and how they misjudge risk. In perfect-information games, everything is visible to both players. You know each other's positions, resources, and potential moves. Chess and Go are classic examples of this approach. The clarity makes skill the main driver of outcomes: the better you anticipate your opponent and the more precise your calculation, the more you deserve to win. The downside is that with everything visible, experienced players can thrive on deep optimization and long converging lines. New players may feel overwhelmed by the depth of forecasting, and a game can become a marathon of perfect plays.

When information is hidden, the game introduces a layer of uncertainty that changes how you think. You're sometimes forced to guess what the opponent might hold or plan around a risk that isn't fully revealed yet. Hidden information can spark bluffing, misdirection, and clever partial information games where you must decide not only what to do, but how much to show. This twist can level the playing field between beginners and veterans, because success hinges as much on reading partial signals as on calculating exact outcomes.

Two micro-cases illustrate the contrast. Case A uses perfect information: you look at the entire board, all markers, all possible future moves, and you must decide the best sequence several steps ahead. Your mind runs through multiple branches, comparing lines of play and pruning unlikely outcomes. Case B relies on hidden information: each player has access to only part of the board or a subset of options, while some details stay concealed. You must reason about what you don't know, tolerate some guesswork, and adjust as new information surfaces. This makes the first glance of the board less revealing, but the moment you reveal a clue or uncover a consequence, you feel a distinct surge of insight.

Design-wise, think about what kind of cognitive load you want. Perfect information tends to favor precision; hidden information invites risk assessment and psychological pacing. If your aim is quick learning and high accessibility, you might lean toward imperfect information with transparent rules that explain how information affects decisions. If your goal is depth and replayability, a well-crafted element of hidden information can be a powerful engine for long-term interest. Either way, you should clearly state what players can and cannot know at each stage, and build your rules around how knowledge changes throughout play.

You can also create graceful transitions between the two extremes. A game might start with hidden information that becomes gradually revealed as the game progresses, or a puzzle might begin with complete visibility but introduce a hidden element that unlocks later. When testing, observe how players talk about what they know and what they fear they don't know. If confusion becomes common, tighten the communication in the rules or adjust the timing so players can feel confident about what they can deduce and when they should hedge their bets.

In practice, your goal is to ensure players have enough information to think clearly, but not so much that they stop exploring new possibilities. Information design should reward curious, patient minds and avoid penalizing beginners for missing a hidden detail. When you strike that balance, your abstract game invites both steady calculation and imaginative exploration.

Determinism and randomness: balancing predictability and surprise

Deterministic games let you see the direct consequences of every choice. If you move a piece here, a line opens or closes there, and the result follows inevitably from the action you took. This clarity helps you learn quickly: you repeat the kind of moves that lead to favorable outcomes, and you can measure progress by whether your planning improves. The downside is that with full determinism, clever players can force long, predictable sequences that feel less dynamic over time. The heart of the challenge becomes avoiding rote repetition and finding fresh paths within a fixed system.

Some games introduce randomness to shake things up. Randomness can be as simple as rolling a die, drawing a card, or shuffling starting positions. The spark of unpredictability makes each game feel different and can create opportunities for outright surprise. The flip side is that luck can overshadow skill, which may frustrate players who want a steady measuring stick for improvement. A well-balanced blend keeps the game fair and exciting: skill remains the main driver, but luck can tilt the odds enough to create new chances without ruining strategic growth.

Two micro-cases show the spectrum. Case A is a deterministic setup: on your turn you choose a move, and the outcome follows from those choices. You learn by studying patterns and planning several steps ahead, and your results reflect your clear decisions. Case B introduces a dose of randomness: a small chance that a move might have an unexpected but bounded effect, or a random starting arrangement that players must adapt to. This shifts early-game decisions and rewards flexible thinking, while still letting players demonstrate mastery as play proceeds.

When you design, consider how much weight you want to give to luck versus skill. A purely deterministic game is welcoming for players who enjoy deep planning and precision. A game with a touch of randomness can attract players who enjoy variety and repeat play without fear of a single losing line blocking progression. The best designs often rely on a steady hand: predictable mechanics that invite careful exploration, with occasional, carefully constrained surprises that refresh the experience instead of derail it.

In testing, keep an eye on whether outcomes feel fair across many plays. If luck dominates a lot of results, you may need to tighten the randomness or add safe guides that help players recover from bad draws. If skilled play always overpowers luck, you might introduce minor, carefully placed uncertainties to keep the game lively without eroding mastery. The right balance gives you a game that remains accessible for newcomers while still offering meaningful, repeatable depth for seasoned players.

Key Takeaway: In abstract design, you shape how players think and feel by controlling turn rhythm, visibility, and the role of chance. The right mix invites clear, clever planning, maintains a fair sense of risk, and rewards both thoughtful calculation and adaptable thinking.

Coming up next Subtittle: Building Simple Components

1) Minimal pieces and boards that enable rich play,

2) Designing reusable mechanics and modular parts,

3) Physical affordances and ergonomics for abstract pieces

Chapter 4

Building Simple Components

You will learn to design simple components that unlock deep, strategic play using as few pieces and as little board as possible.

Minimal pieces and boards that enable rich play

Simplicity can be the engine of complexity. When you strip a design down to a few pieces and a small board, the space for clever decisions grows because every move carries more weight. Consider how Go uses a simple set of stones on a grid. The stones are all the same, the board is just intersections, yet the possible patterns explode as players place stones. That's not magic; it's the mathematics of space and influence. When you design with restraint, you invite players to discover subtle aims—blocking, surrounding, eyeing territory—without needing a long list of special rules or flashy gimmicks. Your goal is to create a canvas where a handful of pieces can generate a vast, unfolding conversation between players.

Start by choosing a board size and a very small set of piece types. A tiny, well-chosen board can amplify strategy more than a huge one with a big ruleset. For example, imagine a compact square board with eight to twelve tokens per side and a single kind of marker for each player. On that stage, every placement matters. Every move becomes a choice about shape, tempo, and future options. The trick is to keep the objective obvious but not trivial. You want players to feel the pull of a long-term plan while they manage immediate threats. In practice, this means aligning the board geometry with the core ideas you want players to explore—territory, control of critical lines, or balance between offense and defense. When the board and pieces fit together, the game teaches you its own language, and players begin speaking it fluently in a few turns.

Two micro-cases help this idea land. In the first, you design a two-player abstract on a 4x4 grid with six tokens per side and no additional pieces. The challenge is to connect your tokens across the center while preventing your opponent from creating a blocking chain. On such a small stage, beginners notice how early tempo decisions set the pace for the rest of the game. The second micro-case involves a circular Mancala-like layout with a handful of stones and a couple of scoring cups. Even with minimal hardware, you can illustrate turn economy: how to convert a single move into two potential gains or how to sacrifice a move now to secure a larger payoff later. These exercises demonstrate that the richness of play lives in how space and timing interact, not in how many pieces you own.

As you prototype, test for readability and equivalence. Can players explain a move in one sentence? Do all pieces feel interchangeable, or do some have subtle specialities that justify their presence? If two pieces seem redundant, you likely don't need both. The reward for trimming is clarity: players spend less time deciphering rules and more time exploring strategy. You can reach deeper play by ensuring every placement, capture, or maneuver creates meaningful choices, even when the board is small and the rules are short.

Two more considerations come into play here: balance and accessibility. If the board size is too small, it can feel cramped; if it's too large, the game loses focus. Test different scales and ask players which feels crisp and which feels wandering. Accessibility means more than legibility of the rules. It includes how easily players can see pieces, distinguish colors, and grasp the basic motions. For example, choose high-contrast colors, use distinct shapes for each side, and keep counters nicely sized so they're easy to pick up and move. Accessibility invites more players to enjoy the game and helps ideas spread through play rather than through instruction.

Designing reusable mechanics and modular parts

Modularity is the heart of flexible design. A modular mechanic is one idea that can be combined with others to create a family of games, or to evolve a single game over time without reinventing the wheel. Start by identifying a core action that matters in every game you want to support—moving, placing, capturing, or pairing—and express it in the simplest possible form. Then ask: how can this action be reused in different contexts? A single rule can become an umbrella for several modes, each with its own flavor but sharing the same DNA.

One strong approach is to create a toolkit of small, interchangeable rules: rotate a piece to indicate a change in status; place a marker to mark influence; move along a grid to extend control in a new direction. Each tool should be neutral enough to apply in multiple situations but distinct enough to alter strategy when combined. The payoff is resilience: your game can be adjusted for complexity, audience, or theme by swapping in different mechanics without rewriting the entire system.

A practical way to test modularity is to draft a short "rule lib" of three to five modules. Keep each module extremely small and well-scoped. For example, module A might say "a player may place one marker per turn"; module B could add "placing a marker adjacent to two enemy markers scores influence," and module C might introduce "once per game, a player may move a marker to a neighboring empty space." If you can recombine A, B, and C to form at least two clearly distinct playstyles with similar effort, your design has good modular potential. The benefit is obvious: you can create variants for teaching, difficulty levels, or different audiences without risking a fresh design from scratch every time.

A second micro-case shows modularity in action. Imagine a tiny game where players use a set of tokens that are identical in shape but differ by a single feature, such as a notch or a dot on the top. The notch could indicate "active" status for that token, moving between "inactive" and "active" changes how the token interacts with the board. Now, you can mix and match tokens with or without active status, creating variants that emphasize different strategies—timing, resource control, or defensive play—while maintaining the same underlying system. The same concept can scale up: you can add new modules that introduce alternative win conditions or scoring methods, all anchored to the same modular core. The key is that your pieces stay coherent and recognizably linked to the core action, so players don't have to relearn the wheel each time.

When you design with modularity, you also gain a valuable tool for playtesting. You can experiment with one module at a time, measuring how it shifts balance and how it changes player decisions. You'll likely discover that some modules invite rich tactical depth but only in certain configurations.

That's a signal to refine those modules or pair them with others that keep the game honest and focused. The broader lesson here is simple: modular design pays off in clarity, adaptability, and longevity. It creates a family of experiences that share a spine, so players recognize the same logic across different skins and scales.

A note on production reality helps here as well. When you're thinking modular, imagine the components in physical form. Are the modular pieces easy to grab, snap together, and swap out? Do the modules feel sturdy when players push, slide, or stack them? If you sketch on cardboard, you quickly see how a module's size and shape affect table presence and readability. The physical affordance of your modules—the way they feel in the hand and on the board—becomes a silent teacher, guiding players toward intuitive use and smooth play.

Physical affordances and ergonomics for abstract pieces

Tactile design matters. The moment a player's finger lands on a piece, you've started shaping their understanding of the game. Give your abstract pieces distinctive, comfortable shapes and sizes. If a token is too small, it becomes fiddly; if it's too large, it clumps on the board. Strive for a comfortable middle ground where players can pick up, place, and move with one fluid motion. Weight helps too. A piece that's too light can feel insubstantial; a piece that's too heavy can dominate the table. A balanced weight feels substantial but not overpowering, like a tool you trust to do its job without distraction.

Texture and surface matter as well. A smooth, matte finish reduces glare and makes sliding pieces predictable. A tactile cue—perhaps a raised edge or a groove on one side—helps players distinguish pieces by touch, not just sight. This is especially valuable in low-light rooms or for players with different color-perception needs. You don't want a rule to depend on a color you can't see in a moment of action; you want shape, size, and texture to carry meaning.

Readability on the board is another important ergonomic choice. Use a clear grid or layout, large enough spaces to keep pieces from crowding, and a simple, legible font for any markers. If your game uses numbers or letters to track states, make them easy to read at a glance. Consider accessibility from the start: colorblind-friendly palettes and high-contrast marks help everyone join the game with confidence. A well-designed board invites fast setup, quick grasp, and long, enjoyable sessions.

A practical example. Suppose you're prototyping a tiny strategy game on a 5x5 grid with five tokens per side and two types of markers to track different statuses. You decide to use rounded, slightly heavier tokens for players and a flat, lighter marker for status changes. The rounded tokens are easy to grab and move without tipping, while the lighter marker sits flush on the board so it doesn't feel intrusive. This combination makes the game pleasant to handle, reduces setup fatigue, and keeps the focus on strategy rather than on wrestling with hardware.

As you iterate, ask three quick questions after every prototype session: Do players know where everything belongs on the board at a glance? Is every move readable in the moment, without counting on memory or notes? Do the pieces' shapes and sizes feel appropriate for the pace and scale you're aiming for? If the answer to any is no, adjust the shapes, sizes, or layout. Your goal is for the moment of play to feel natural—the mechanics, the pieces, and the board all disappear into the experience, letting players focus on strategy.

Coming up next

Key Takeaway: You can unlock deep strategy with a tiny toolkit of well-chosen pieces, a compact board, and carefully designed handling that invites clear, quick understanding.

Coming up next Subtittle: Rule Systems and Clarity

1) Writing precise, unambiguous rules ,

2) Edge cases and resolution procedures,

3) Tutorial sequencing: teaching mechanics without theme.

Chapter 5

Rule Systems and Clarity

You will learn to write rules that are precise, unambiguous, and easy to teach, so players can focus on strategy rather than guesswork.

1) Writing precise, unambiguous rules

Define actions with exact verbs and clear conditions. Use one verb per action and stick to it across the entire ruleset. If you say “move,” explain where you may move, what the destination must look like, and what happens to the piece you move. Do not mix terms like “advance,” “step,” or “shift” unless you immediately define them as synonyms of the same action. When in doubt, restate the action in plain language and then state it again in formal terms. The goal is to reduce room for interpretation. A tiny ambiguity can change a game’s outcome in subtle but important ways, so every term should be spell-checked against all rules for consistency.

Clarify permitted moves by listing conditions in sequence. Start with the simplest condition and add constraints one by one, so a reader can check every condition in order without backtracking. For example, say: "A piece may move to an orthogonally adjacent square if that square is empty and not blocked by a rule." If you introduce exceptions, flag them early and tie them to the base rule rather than scattering them later. If two rules could apply to the same action, state which rule takes precedence and why. This clarity saves arguments during playtesting and makes it easier to teach.

Use consistent terminology and avoid synonyms that could confuse players. If you call a thing a "space" in one rule, don't call it a "cell" in another rule unless you immediately declare them equivalent. When you must introduce a new term, define it in the same breath and show a quick example using it. Consistency is the quiet engine of understanding—players won't notice it when it's smooth, but they'll feel the friction when it's off.

Example 1: In a small grid game, you define "move" as "change the position of a piece to any orthogonally adjacent square that is empty." You do not also permit "sliding" or "pushing" unless you describe those actions separately with their own rules. This keeps players from wondering whether a different verb means the same thing.

Example 2: Suppose your rulebook uses "capture" in one place and "eliminate" in another. If you intend them to be the same action, rewrite to use one term consistently or add a precise cross-reference: "capture equals elimination of the opponent's piece by occupying its square." If you need both terms, define them distinctly and show a short example of each usage.

2) Edge cases and resolution procedures

Anticipate the odd, the rare, and the contradictory. Start by listing possible situations that could destabilize a rule—what if two moves happen at once? what if a movement would land you in a forbidden zone? what if a rule conflicts with another rule in a specific layout? Document these as edge cases with a simple, testable rule. If an edge case could derail play, provide a clear resolution method up front. This reduces arguments at the table and speeds up learning.

Specify a clear resolution order or priority for conflicting rules. If two rules could apply to the same situation, tell players which one wins and why. If the order depends on context, give the context: "in a setup phase, Rule A applies; during play, Rule B applies." When you cannot decide on one priority, use a simple tie-break mechanism that is easy to apply during play, such as a default action, or a mutual-stop to discuss and then resume. The key is to keep the path from rule to outcome straightforward.

Document defaults and overrides. Defaults cover the common situations; overrides handle the unusual ones. If a rule says “most of the time X is allowed,” specify what happens when X is not allowed and what the fallback is. This keeps the game predictable and fair. If you introduce an override later in the rules, restate the default first and then show how the override changes the outcome. Players should be able to locate the base behavior quickly and then scan for the exceptions.

Two micro-cases illustrate edge-case thinking. Case A: Two players attempt to move into the same square on the same turn. Your rule could specify that the player who announced the move first wins the right to that square, or you could declare a resolve-by-random-choice option if both moves are declared simultaneously. Either approach should be stated explicitly, with a short rationale so players understand the reason behind it. Case B: A rule creates a situation that looks like it should be allowed but would make the game unbalanced. Your fix should be to add a narrowly scoped constraint rather than a broad rewrite of the entire rule set. Explain the balance intention briefly so learners see why the constraint exists.

3) Tutorial sequencing: teaching mechanics without theme

Break down the mechanics into teachable, non-thematic chunks. The aim is to teach the underlying mechanics in the simplest possible order, so players build understanding step by step. Start with the most essential actions, then introduce only the necessary supporting rules. As you add each chunk, pause to test, refactor, and clarify. A well-structured sequence makes players feel capable early, which motivates deeper experimentation later.

Disclose rules progressively with concrete, minimal examples. Use short, concrete demonstrations that show the rule in action, then invite players to try their own quick variations. If you can teach a rule in two lines plus one quick example, you'll keep attention and avoid information overload. Progress the examples in increasing complexity, but always tie back to the core rule you're teaching. The pointer for learners is: if you can demonstrate it once, you can explain it clearly; if you must repeat, you probably need a more precise wording.

Anchor teaching through short practice plays that reinforce the rule. After explaining a rule, give players a low-stakes practice round that confines choices to the new mechanic. Keep the practice round short, then discuss what happened in plain terms: what worked, what didn't, and why. The aim is to convert abstract wording into embodied understanding. If a learner struggles, slow down, restate the rule in different words, and demonstrate with a fresh example.

Two practical micro-cases show effective sequencing. Case 1: Teach "move" first in a tiny grid where only one move is available per turn. After the student internalizes that action, introduce the condition that squares must be empty. Case 2: Teach "resolve" after learners can move; present an edge-case scenario where two moves collide and show how the resolution rule applies, step by step.

In both cases, the teaching flow keeps the thematic glaze off the mechanics, letting the logic shine.

Key Takeaway: Clear, consistent rules and deliberate edge-case handling aren't just good practice—they're the backbone of fair, teachable games that players can master quickly.

Coming up next: Designing for Depth and Elegance

1) Emergent complexity from simple rules

2) Creating meaningful decisions every turn

3) Avoiding dominant strategies and trivial play

You'll see how simple, well-balanced rules can generate rich, surprising gameplay, and you'll learn to guide players toward decisions that matter in every move. In the next chapter, we'll explore how depth grows from elegant beginnings and how to keep the play interesting for both new and seasoned players.

Chapter 6

Designing for Depth and Elegance

By the end of this chapter you will know how to design abstract games that grow depth from simple rules, ensure every turn offers a meaningful decision, and avoid dull, overpowered ideas.

Emergent complexity from simple rules

Abstract games often start with a small rule set, then surprise you with how much strategy hides inside. The core idea is simple: you give players a few finite actions, a shared space to act in, and a clear win condition. From there, players explore the space, and patterns emerge without you adding more pieces or stories. This is not magic; it is the maths of choice under constraint. When rules are tight and the board or pieces are consistent, every move reshapes what counts as a good move a few turns later. The depth you see is a product of interaction, not of clever backstory.

Two brief examples help illustrate the point without needing special jargon. In a small grid game, players place markers on empty intersections. The only goal is to capture or control spaces, but the choice of where to place a marker matters not just for this moment but for the possibilities it opens or closes in the future. A move near the center can affect multiple lines of play, while a move on the edge changes fewer options. The tension arises as each player must weigh immediate gains against long-term risk, because a single placement can enable a future trap or a hard-to-defend position. The outcome isn't decided by a single clever move, but by a sequence of choices where early decisions constrain later ones.

In another tiny example, imagine a game where moving a piece creates new possibilities for both players and sometimes blocks the opponent's best options. The rule set remains small, yet players discover multiple paths to victory: aggressive play, slow accumulation, or quiet preparation that pays off later. Because the board state changes in nuanced ways with each move, there isn't a single "best" plan that stays best no matter what the other player does. Emergent depth appears as you navigate this evolving map of opportunities and threats, not as a trick you add to the game.

What makes this work is clarity plus constraint. The rules must be exact enough to avoid endless argument, and the board layout or piece behavior must be predictable enough that players can map consequences from one move to the next. If rules are vague, players lose the sense that their decisions matter. If the board is too free or the pieces too powerful, games slide into guessing and luck rather than skill. When you design, aim for a balance where small, local choices propagate into meaningful global structures. The result feels surprising yet fair, and players walk away with that "aha" moment when a simple move unlocks a deeper line of play.

A practical way to test emergent complexity is to watch for how many distinct plans players develop after only a few rounds. If both players converge quickly on the same sequence of moves, the game may be too constrained or too predictable. If players consistently discover new, plausible strategies across sessions, the rule set is producing genuine depth. You're looking for a spectrum of viable approaches, not a single optimal script. Emergent depth should feel like a garden you tend: small, well-kept rules that generate an ever-shifting landscape.

Creating meaningful decisions every turn

A game shines when every turn offers a choice that matters, not just a routine placement or a coin toss. Meaningful decisions are about tradeoffs: you weigh short-term gains against longer-term outcomes, you anticipate the opponent's responses, and you accept that some decisions close doors while opening others. When decisions accumulate across turns, the game becomes a conversation rather than a sequence of isolated actions.

One way to build meaningful choices is to structure move options so that each option carries clearer future implications. For example, a move might grant you a local advantage now but reveal a vulnerability later on, or it may strengthen a position you've invested in, while weakening a parallel option you could have pursued. The key is to connect present choices to future states in a way players can imagine, even if they cannot predict every twist.

Two micro-cases make this concrete. In the first, consider a game where you can claim a space or block an opponent's potential line. Claiming space gives you immediate control, but blocking a line might restrict the opponent's future options more than it boosts your own. The best move is often the one that preserves options for several turns, not just the one that yields the most points right now. The second case involves tempo—the rhythm of play. You might choose a move that speeds up the game to push the opponent into a rushed decision, or you might slow down to keep control of the board and force the other player to pick a path they don't love. Each decision is a thread in a larger tapestry; pull on one thread, and you'll notice how it changes the whole picture.

To keep decisions meaningful, you also need to limit "free wins." If a single move always leads to a guaranteed victory, players will circle around that move and ignore everything else. That's boring and uncreative. Instead, design counterplay into the system. Add rules that reward different kinds of expertise: tactical calculation, long-term planning, or positional accuracy. When players have multiple decent avenues to victory, the game remains engaging turn after turn. The best moments come when one player notices a subtle line of play that hinges on a small detail—like a timing window, a forced sequence, or an overlooked interaction between two rules.

A simple practical check: play several rounds with a friend, then switch to another partner. If both partners consistently feel they could have improved their play by making the same kinds of moves, you may need to adjust the balance so different lines stay viable. If, instead, you notice a few moves always dominate, you probably have a dominant strategy creeping in. In either case, use the feedback to refine the rule set so that each turn remains a real puzzle rather than a fixed script.

Avoiding dominant strategies and trivial play

A game becomes dull when one move, one approach, or one piece always leads to the same result, regardless of the opponent's plan. Dominant strategies strip away choice and reduce play to a single path. Trivial play happens when the game invites the same safe, predictable response every time, so players can finish a match with little variation. Both issues sap the joy of learning and the satisfaction of mastery.

To prevent this, design for variety and counterplay. Here are several practical ideas that keep the game lively without sacrificing fairness. First, introduce asymmetry. If each player has identical powers, the first-move advantage can tilt balance unless carefully countered. Asymmetry can be as simple as giving one side a slightly different starting position, a different movement option, or a unique resource flow. The goal is to create legitimate but non-dominant paths to victory for both sides.

Second, limit unconditional power. If a move can always be used to win outright, it will be exploited. Consider adding a cost to powerful moves, a risk if you overuse them, or a timing window where the move is particularly strong but fleeting. The timing window forces players to think about when a move is worth the risk, not just if it exists.

Third, build counterplay into the rules. A strong move should invite a direct response that neutralizes it or shifts the balance in the opponent's favor. Counterplay makes both players think more carefully. If every good move softens the same line of defense, your game will feel formulaic; if each good move opens a new set of responses, the game stays fresh.

Fourth, use information structure to avoid perfect foresight. Perfect information—where both players can see everything at all times—can lead to long, deterministic races. Hidden information or partial visibility can force players to make decisions with incomplete data, which adds texture and tension. The same rule applies to randomness: a little unpredictability can prevent stalemates, but too much randomness erodes skill. The trick is to keep a balance where skill still wins most of the time, but the path to victory isn't a straight line.

Finally, maintain a tight rule set. If rules grow too complex, players may derive the best path by memorizing long sequences rather than understanding underlying strategy. Clear, precise rules help players focus on thinking rather than decoding how the game works. Regular playtests focused on rule clarity—checking whether players interpret a rule the same way—reduce confusion and keep the play experience fair.

In practice, you'll often iterate in small steps. After a round, ask what decision felt pivotal and why. If a single choice repeatedly dictates the outcome, reexamine that move's power, timing, and its interactions with other rules. If the game seems to reward random luck more than skill, introduce balancing adjustments or more meaningful non-deterministic elements. The aim is to preserve a range of valid strategies while curbing any single path from dominating.

With depth, meaningful decisions, and robust balance, your abstract game can stay compelling across many sessions. Players should feel that clever, well-thought-out play consistently pays off, but that a clever counterplay exists for every strong idea. That dialogue between intention and response—the core of strategic play—lives in the tiny choices you design and the way those choices interact on the board.

Coming up next: Subtittle: Balancing and Playtesting

1) Metrics for balance: symmetry, first-player advantage, tempo

2) Systematic playtest methods and iteration cycles

3) Collecting and interpreting player data qualitatively and quantitatively

Key Takeaway: Depth grows from small, well-crafted rules, and every turn should offer a decision that matters, not a routine move that could be skipped.

Coming up next, Subtittle: Balancing and Playtesting, where you will learn how to measure balance, test ideas with real players, and read what the data says to improve your designs.

Chapter 7

Balancing and Playtesting

You will learn how to measure balance in a game, run focused playtests, and translate what you observe into concrete design tweaks.

Metrics for balance: symmetry, first-player advantage, tempo

Balance in abstract game design means every reasonable move has a corresponding counter, every piece has a fair role, and no single choice dominates the entire game. You want players to feel they choose, not to feel trapped by a single winning path. Start by thinking about three core metrics: symmetry, first-player advantage, and tempo.

Step 1: Define symmetry in your game. Symmetry means that the game offers comparable options for both players, often achieved with mirrored boards, mirrored pieces, or rules that give each side equivalent opportunities. If you test a symmetric setup, you should see that, when both players play well, neither side has an intrinsic edge baked into the design. Rationale: symmetry is the backbone of fair play in abstract games. If a setup unfairly rewards one color, piece, or starting position, players will notice and the fun drains away.

Step 2: Check first-player advantage and how to measure it. In many abstract games, the player who moves first can gain initiative. That's not always bad, but it should be deliberate and balanced. To check it, play multiple rounds with swapping starting positions. If the starting player wins far more often than not, you likely need a fix—perhaps a rule that gives the second player a compensating option, or a more balanced starting layout. Rationale: if one side always has the edge simply because they move first, players will learn to avoid the game or feel it's about who goes first, not who plays best.

Step 3: Gauge tempo and the pace of decisions. Tempo is about how quickly meaningful choices arrive and how often a game reaches a decisive moment. A game that moves too slowly can bore, while one that collapses in a few moves can feel unsatisfying or unfair. To gauge tempo, watch how often players reach critical decisions, how long each decision takes, and whether games tend to end in a flurry or a slow grind. If early moves routinely lock in a win, the tempo is too predictable; if late-game swings never happen, the tempo may be too slow. Rationale: balanced tempo keeps both players engaged, creates tension at the right moments, and allows clever ideas to shine rather than luck or rule quirks.

Two short micro-cases to see these ideas in action

Micro-case A: You run a small, mirrored grid game with identical pieces and rules for both sides. In a handful of sessions, you notice that the first player consistently wins when both players play optimally. You split the group and run half the games with the second player starting. The win rate evens out only when the second starter receives a small, clearly defined compensating option—say, a slightly weaker first move or a move that unlocks a limited response. Principle: if first-player advantage exists, introduce a balanced counter or equalize options to restore fairness without erasing strategy.

Micro-case B: In a fast, nearly instantaneous tactical game, games often end within the first five moves. Decisions feel sharp, but players barely have time to test options. You introduce a small change: a second set of legal responses becomes available after the fourth move, lengthening the decision tree just enough to create meaningful choices without dragging the pace. Result: players notice new paths, the tempo remains brisk, and the edge shifts from "who blinks first" to "who sees the right sequence." Principle: adjust tempo so decisions occur at a cadence that rewards planning and discovery, not mere occurrence of a fast finish.

Systematic playtest methods and iteration cycles

A solid playtest plan is a map of how you'll learn from players, what you'll change, and how you'll measure progress. The goal is to learn fast, with a clear question in mind for each round.

Step 4: Plan a focused playtest plan with a single question. Before you gather players, write down one clear question you want to answer in this round. For example: "Does the current symmetry break a widespread first-move advantage without creating new imbalances?" Or: "Does the proposed tempo change improve engagement without slowing the game too much?" Having one question keeps your observations sharp and your changes targeted. Rationale: a focused question helps you stay objective and makes the data easier to interpret.

Step 5: Run repeatable rounds with consistent conditions. Use a small, repeatable setup: the same board, the same starting positions, the same timer or turn structure. Have a standard script for the session: explain the rules, run a few practice moves, then begin the real test, record outcomes, and finish with a quick debrief. Repetition matters because it reduces noise. Rationale: controlled conditions let you compare results across sessions and identify real effects of changes rather than random variation.

Step 6: Iterate by changing one variable at a time and re-test. After each round of data, adjust only one aspect of the design—perhaps the starting option, or the strength of a particular move, or the timing constraint. Then run a new set of sessions to see whether the change moves the needle toward your test question's goal. Rationale: single-variable iteration helps you map cause and effect clearly. If you change multiple things at once, you'll struggle to know which tweak did what.

Two micro-cases to illustrate the process

Micro-case C: You test a rule tweak that adds a second-mark influence after a certain move, hoping to rebalance first-move balance. You conduct five rounds, switching who starts each time. You collect data on who wins under each condition and note players' subjective sense of fairness. Result: you can see whether the tweak reduces the edge of moving first, while not introducing new biases elsewhere.

Micro-case D: You time-box decisions more strictly to see whether tempo improves engagement. You run sessions with a fixed time per move and compare to a control group with looser timing. Result: players report that choices feel crisper, and the overall game pace remains lively without dragging. Principle: timing constraints can adjust tempo in predictable ways when applied consistently.

Collecting and interpreting player data qualitatively and quantitatively

Good design grows from both numbers and narratives. You want to capture what players did, what they felt, and what patterns show up across many sessions. Do both, but keep the data manageable.

Step 7: Collect data with simple, repeatable methods. Use a lightweight form after each session: record the winner, any moves that seemed pivotal, and a short note about what felt fair or unfair. For the qualitative side, ask players what surprised them, what felt obvious, and where they felt stuck. For the quantitative side, tally outcomes by starting player, by move lengths, by which moves were most common, and by decisive moments. Rationale: numerical signals plus player stories together reveal both the shape of the balance and the human feel of the game.

Step 8: Look for patterns in decisions and outcomes. Review your notes to identify recurring themes: are players consistently choosing particular moves, do certain sequences end games quickly, or do some rules produce unusual deadlocks? Patterns point to underlying properties of the system—symmetry, balance, and flow. Rationale: patterns help you separate stray incidents from real dynamics you should address.

Step 9: Translate findings into concrete changes and test again. Write a short design note for each change you want to try, explain why you think it will help, and set a deadline for the next round of testing. Then re-run the playtests with the same careful controls. Rationale: you want a living design that improves with evidence, not a collection of guesses.

Two micro-cases to see data in action

Micro-case E: After a session, several players say they felt the game was "decided early" but not "clear why." You flag a few early actions as key decision points and propose an adjustment to either highlight those decisions or adjust their consequences. You test with a fixed scenario and gather new data; the feedback confirms whether the change clarified the early dynamics.

Micro-case F: You notice a strong preference for a particular sequence that outdoors even in different variants, suggesting a hidden bias in the rules. You adjust the wording of a rule and slightly rebalance the effect of a move to remove the bias. You test again and find a more even distribution of outcomes. Principle: players' impressions matter; data confirms whether those impressions reflect real system behavior.

Key Takeaway: Balance comes from clear questions, controlled testing, and changes that target the root of imbalance, not just symptoms.

Coming up next: Pacing and Player Experience

Subtittle: Pacing and Player Experience

1) Session length and satisfying game loops,

2) Tension curves and comeback mechanics,

3) Accessibility and cognitive load management

Chapter 8

Pacing and Player Experience

By the end of this chapter you will be able to plan game pacing that keeps players engaged from start to finish, balancing how long a game lasts, how tension builds and eases, and how to make rules accessible for younger players and newcomers.

1) Session length and satisfying game loops

You want players to feel a complete experience in a single sitting. A good starting target for many ages is something around 15 to 25 minutes, but the exact window depends on your players and the game's complexity. The core idea is a loop: a simple sequence of actions that players repeat, learn from, and then adjust as the game moves toward a finish. Think of a loop as a small rhythm you can hear in your game: plan, act, respond, score or reset a bit, then do it again with new information.

Identify the core loop quickly. What does a player do on their turn that matters for the overall outcome? If the loop has too many tiny steps, you risk slowing the pace; if it's too blunt, players might finish too fast and miss meaningful decisions. For a beginner-friendly abstract design, keep the loop tight and clear: one or two decisions per turn, immediate feedback, and a clear moment when the loop ends and scoring tallies or new phases begin.

A simple way to shape the loop is to map one complete cycle: choose an action, see the result, note what changes on the board or in your options, and then pass to the next player. If a typical loop takes about one minute, a 20-minute session can have roughly 15–20 loops, which gives players enough chances to see cause and effect without getting bored or overwhelmed.

Example 1: A two-player abstract game in a casual setting. The core loop is: on your turn, you place a piece, then you remove or move another piece according to a simple rule. The loop repeats, with each move visibly shifting the balance of power. The session finishes when a simple target condition is met (for example, a player achieves a specific alignment or blocks an opponent). The result feels deliberate, but the pace stays lively because decisions come quickly and the feedback is immediate.

Example 2: A classroom-friendly variant with a fixed 20-minute clock. Players take turns making a move that earns points if they connect lines in a certain pattern. After a set number of rounds, the board is tallied and the winner is revealed. The loop is short, predictable, and easy to explain, which makes it possible to run several quick rounds in a single class without fatigue or confusion.

Focusing on loops this way helps you predict how long a game will feel and gives you levers to adjust. If players finish too early, shorten the loop by removing an optional step or reducing the number of rounds. If players stall, tighten the decision space or speed up resolution. The goal is a rhythm that feels satisfying and complete, with a clear sense of "we played, we learned, we finished."

2) Tension curves and comeback mechanics

Tension is the feeling of anticipation before a move, a choice, or a reveal that could swing the outcome. It grows when players sense their decisions matter a lot right now and when the game occasionally nudges them toward a comeback or a reversal. To create tension without chaos, design moments where a single move can change the score, position, or possibilities in a noticeable way.

Think in three layers: early setup tension, mid-game pressure, and late-game suspense. Early tension comes from players understanding the game and realizing their first few moves shape the long path. Mid-game tension grows as options narrow or the board shows a clear trend. Late-game tension peaks when a last chance decision could flip the result.

Comeback mechanics give players a fair shot to recover from a mistake or shift momentum near the end. They should be accessible, not gimmicks. A good comeback mechanic creates a final surge rather than an abrupt, unfair swing. For example, you can provide a small amount of late-scoring potential that only activates in the last few turns, or you can grant a narrow window where a clever sequence unlocks extra points. The key is to reward smart play without invalidating earlier effort.

Micro-case 1: In a mid-game swing, a player holds back a resource for a crucial late move. The other player takes the lead, but as the clock nears the end, the first player gains just enough advantage from a single, well-timed move to turn the tide. The satisfaction comes from seeing a small, careful decision become decisive when time runs out.

Micro-case 2: A late-score boost opens only if players complete a specific pattern within the final rounds. This creates a suspenseful finish: players know the pattern is within reach but only a precise sequence will unlock it. Even if you miss it, the game ends with a clear and fair conclusion, and players leave with a sense that timing mattered.

To maintain healthy tension, balance visibility and surprise. If every important move is obvious, players feel confident too early and the game loses suspense. If information is hidden or outcomes are unpredictable, players may feel frustrated rather than challenged. The goal is a steady stream of meaningful choices where the best move isn't always obvious, but the correct path is learnable with practice.

3) Accessibility and cognitive load management

Accessibility means making the game easy to learn and enjoyable for a wide range of players. Cognitive load is the mental effort required to understand rules, remember constraints, and plan moves. You can lower cognitive load without dulling the game by using simple, consistent rules, clear symbol systems, and concise explanations.

Start with a small rule set. If players can recite the core loop and the win condition after a short demonstration, you're in a good place. Use consistent actions and predictable patterns. If a piece type exists, give it a predictable role; if a rule exists, explain it with a single example and one or two quick reminders on the board. Visuals should be legible: pieces that share shape or color should be easy to tell apart for players with normal vision, and accessible color palettes help players who have color vision differences.

Create a friendly tutorial path. Build a quick-start guide that covers the three simplest moves and the ending condition. Then add one or two "gotchas" that often cause confusion, paired with a short reminder to consult the rule sheet. The aim is to allow someone to play within minutes, then gradually uncover deeper rules as they gain confidence.

Example 3: A family puzzle game uses five simple pieces and two colors. The rule sheet uses large, bold icons to show each action, with a short one-line caption under each icon. During the first play, new players complete all three instructions on the sheet and finish a test round in under 10 minutes. They then read a longer explanation to learn optional expansions, but the core play remains approachable.

Example 4: A classroom variant with step-by-step diagrams. The teacher presents a two-page flowchart that shows what to do on each turn, what happens when a line is completed, and how scoring works. Students can reference the diagram during play, reducing the need to memorize every rule from memory. The result is less confusion and more time for meaningful decisions.

With accessibility, you'll build a game that invites people to try it without fear of getting stuck in the rules. You'll also create opportunities for players with different learning styles to engage: some will prefer quick, concrete actions; others will enjoy reading a short, illustrated guide. The important point is to test with diverse players and notice where they stumble. If a group consistently asks for a hint after a specific rule, consider a clearer explanation or a simplified version for that rule.

Examples and micro-cases in action

Example A: A two-player loop game uses a simple "place and respond" mechanic. You place a marker, the other player places a marker, and then you both resolve a small scoring event. The loop repeats until a timer ends. Players learn quickly, and the session ends with a clear winner, keeping momentum high.

Example B: A family-friendly game adds a late-game scoring boost that unlocks only in the last three turns. This creates a dramatic finish while keeping early and mid-game decisions meaningful. The players feel the tension rise as the clock winds down, and the outcome isn't known until the last move.

Exercises

1) Play a 20-minute draft of your game with a friend. Note how many loops fit into the time, how long each loop lasts, and where players lose focus. After playing, answer: Was the session length comfortable? Did the loop feel engaging across turns?

2) Run a short 10-minute test focusing on tension. Observe when players feel drawn to make big moves and when they play it safe. Mark two moments when tension correctly rose and two moments when it dropped. Adjust the loop so tension rises at those pivotal points.

3) Do a 15-minute accessibility check. Have someone explain the core loop in one minute and then try to play once without looking at the full rule book. Note where they stumble most and simplify those two areas. Record what changes reduced confusion.

Troubleshooting

- If sessions feel too long or too short, re-check your target loop frequency and turn length. Shorten or extend a loop by removing or adding a single action per turn.

- If players don't feel tension, review whether the end condition is too easy or if feedback from moves is too subtle. Increase visibility of the effect of key moves or introduce a late-game reward that is noticeable but not overpowering.

- If players struggle with rules, add a one-page quick-start sheet and create a short glossary with only the most-used terms. Consider a visual cheat sheet that shows the core loop with three icons and captions.

- If comeback mechanics feel unfair, ensure late-game options are available to both players and that the swing is proportional to the game state, not to a single lucky move. Test with a few rounds and adjust the scoring or triggers so the final moments feel earned.

Tools and templates you can copy

- Session Planner Template

Game name:

Target session length (minutes):

Core loop actions (three bullets):

Turn cadence (how long each turn should take):

End condition (how the game ends):

Accessibility notes (keys to quick learning):

- Quick Start Rule Sheet Template

Rule 1: Core loop (one-line summary)

Rule 2: End condition

Rule 3: First three player actions (with tiny diagrams)

Rule 4: One example move sequence (two lines)

- Playtest Log Template

Date:

Players:

Observed loop length (average seconds per loop):

Tension notes (moments of rise/fall):

Confusions or rule questions:

Adjustments made (before next test):

Key Takeaway: Good pacing means a clear, repeatable loop that fits comfortably in the target time, balanced by moments of tension and a mild path to comeback, all presented in a way that new players can grasp quickly.

Coming up next

Subtittle: Computational Tools and Analysis

1) Simulations, AI opponents, and Monte Carlo evaluations,

2) Game trees, state space reduction, and solvability,

3) Using software to refine balance and discover emergent tactics.

Chapter 9

Computational Tools and Analysis

You want to test your abstract game quickly, see where balance breaks, and spot emergent tactics without waiting for a long string of human games. Do this by combining simple simulations, friendly AI opponents, and Monte Carlo evaluations. The idea is to learn what actually happens when two players play many times under controlled conditions, so you can tune rules and balance before moving to bigger playtests.

Step 1: Define what you're measuring. Decide what "balanced" or "good play" means for your game. Is the first move a slight advantage, or can the game be equally winnable from different openings? Pick 2–3 clear metrics to track, such as win rate by opening move, average number of turns to finish, and how often the board reaches a critical decision point. Rationale: clear goals keep your simulations useful and not just noisy data.

Step 2: Build a simple test harness. Create a minimal version of your rules that runs in your favorite tool or a basic script. It doesn't need art or fancy UI—just the moves, the board, and a way to play out turns. Rationale: a lean harness runs fast, lets you focus on the logic, and makes it easy to run many trials.

Step 3: Start with random play to establish a baseline. Have both sides pick legal moves at random for a large number of games. Record outcomes and timing. Rationale: random play reveals the raw structure of the game—where the game naturally leans toward one side, what moves tend to appear, and how often it reaches decisive moments.

Step 4: Add a basic AI opponent. Implement a straightforward heuristic and let it play against a human-like partner. For example, prefer moves that increase your control over a key zone or reduce your opponent's immediate options. Rationale: a simple AI helps you see how the game behaves when decisions aren't random, without needing heavy programming.

Step 5: Run Monte Carlo evaluations. For each position, simulate many random playouts from that position and tally which side tends to win. Use the results to infer which moves or positions have higher probability of success. Rationale: Monte Carlo methods give a probabilistic sense of the strength of moves, even if the rules are too complex for exact calculation.

Step 6: Analyze and act. Look at where the data clusters. Do certain openings dominate, or do particular board configurations exhaust a player's options too quickly? Identify a few rules or balance knobs to adjust (for example, move costs, capture rules, or space control) and test the effect by re-running simulations. Rationale: data guides where to tune parameters, saving time in human testing.

Example 1: Imagine a tiny 4x4 board game with a few tokens and capture mechanics. You run 5,000 random games to map the baseline, then drop in a simple AI that tends to occupy the center and push toward the corners. After 2,000 Monte Carlo playouts from various mid-game positions, you notice central control rarely wins easily, but controlling a particular corner increases win rates by a meaningful margin. You adjust the corner value and re-run simulations to confirm the change nudges outcomes toward more varied strategic paths.

Example 2: Consider a game where players alternately place stones, with a rule that forbids repeating a previous board state. You introduce an AI that favors moves creating diverse, nonredundant positions. Monte Carlo tests show a reduction in repetitive cycles and more decisive games. You refine the rule to encourage exploration without letting outcomes drift too far toward one gimmick. The data shows players experience a wider range of tactics, which you then validate with short human sessions.

Troubleshooting and quick fixes:

- If results are noisy, increase the number of trials or seed the random generator to reduce variance.

- If the AI seems too weak or too strong, tune the scoring heuristic a few points at a time and re-run tests.

- If Monte Carlo playouts lean toward a single move, adjust the move weighting so less-explored paths get a chance.

- If you see bias from the harness itself (like a bug in how moves are generated), run a separate checker that validates every move's legality in random samples.

- If balance looks good in simulation but terrible in real play, expand the AI variety to include more human-like strategies during testing.

Tools and templates you can copy:

- A simple test harness outline: set up the board, define legal moves, apply a move, switch players, check end conditions, log results.

- A basic balance log template: position, move suggested, Monte Carlo win rate, confidence (based on sample size), notes.

- A Monte Carlo runner template: loop over trials, apply random playouts, record outcomes, compute win rates and standard errors.

Two short micro-cases to clarify the process:

- Micro-case A: You test a move that claims a new territory. Monte Carlo results show it wins more often in openings that involve early expansion, but loses value in late-game positions. You alter the rule to limit early expansion a touch, then re-run trials to verify the effect.

- Micro-case B: An AI that always prioritizes parity of moves produces longer, more predictable games. You introduce a small bias toward diversification of move types, reducing stalemates and increasing tactical diversity, then check if the new approach sustains balance across many games.

Key takeaways and quick checks:

- Monte Carlo evaluations give probabilistic insights into move strength and position value, not absolute certainty.

- Start simple: random play, then add a single AI capability, then run many trials to see the effect.

- Use small, fast tests to iterate quickly before committing to broader playtests.

Coming up next Subtittle: Publishing, Community, and Evolving Designs

1) Prototyping to production: art, components, and manufacturing constraints,

2) Building community: rulesets, variants, and tournament formats,

3) Iterative post-release support and evolving metagame

2. Game trees, state space reduction, and solvability

You want to understand how deep the rabbit hole goes in your abstract game. By mapping the game tree, trimming unnecessary branches, and thinking about solvability, you get a clearer sense of how players could master the system and where the design invites clever, non-obvious play.

Step 1: Sketch a map of the game tree. Start with the starting position and list possible moves. From each resulting position, list next moves, and so on, but stop at a practical depth for your study. Rationale: a visual map helps you see how decisions multiply and where the branching becomes unwieldy.

Step 2: Look for symmetries and canonical forms. If two positions are essentially the same under rotation, reflection, or piece relabeling, treat them as identical. Rationale: recognizing symmetry cuts the number of distinct positions you must analyze, speeding up the work and clarifying core decisions.

Step 3: Apply pruning to prune infeasible branches. When a position clearly cannot lead to a better outcome than a found alternative, you can safely ignore it for your purposes. Rationale: pruning keeps you focused on meaningful paths and makes analysis tractable.

Step 4: Consider solvability in principle. Some games are fully solvable for small boards or simplified rules; others remain open questions. You don't need to prove solvability for the full game to gain value—note whether certain positions look decisively winning or losing and how quickly players converge to those outcomes. Rationale: understanding solvable slices informs design choices without requiring heavy theory.

Step 5: Build smaller prototypes to test ideas. Create pared-down versions of the game with fewer pieces or a smaller board to study how the core mechanics behave. Rationale: simpler versions reveal whether the fundamental ideas scale or collapse when complexity grows.

Step 6: Translate findings back into rules. Use your tree and reduction insights to simplify or adjust rules so that depth emerges from the intended decisions rather than from accidental complexity. Rationale: sound rules yield meaningful choices rather than accidental advantage.

Example 1: Take a tiny placement game on a 3x3 grid with a capture rule. The state space is modest, so you can enumerate all positions with a quick script. You notice many positions are mirror images; after collapsing symmetries, the effective space shrinks dramatically. A few turns show a consistent pattern: the first player can force early tempo, but careful defense by the second player neutralizes it. You tweak the capture rule to require a secondary condition for capture, which reduces first-player tempo while preserving interesting mid-game decisions.

Example 2: In a slightly larger variant on a 4x4 board, you test a simplified version where players only place tokens and can't move them later. The reduced scope lets you exhaustively search the early game and identify a handful of safe-but-dull openings. You then reintroduce a movement option in a narrowed form and reassess. The balance shifts from dull to dynamic, and the reduced tree size helps you see where players will find meaningful choices rather than repetitive moves.

Troubleshooting and quick fixes:

- If the state space remains too large, tighten symmetry rules or drop nonessential features to create a first-pass model you can analyze fully.

- If pruning removes potentially valid strategies, review the pruning criteria and test with a broader set of examples to avoid bias.

- If solvability hints are unclear, analyze very small or highly constrained variants first, then gradually scale up while tracking changes.

- If you find contradictory results across depths, triangulate by using multiple depths and comparing outcomes to identify consistent patterns.

Tools and templates you can use:

- A state-space map template: a grid for positions, moves, and outcomes; mark symmetries and canonical forms.

- A pruning checklist: identify clearly losing branches and justify their exclusion.

- A solvability note sheet: lines for “solved? yes/no,” “board size,” “why” and “what it implies for design.”

Two micro-cases to illustrate the process:

- Micro-case C: A 2x3 board with limited moves creates a tiny decision tree that you can fully map. The complete tree reveals a handful of winning lines that reward aggressive early play. You adjust the opening rules to equalize paths and test again.

- Micro-case D: A game that seems balanced on paper collapses on deeper analysis because a small, overlooked symmetry allows a forced win. You remedy by rebalancing a rule so symmetry no longer gives a clean victory path, then re-check with the tree map.

Key takeaways and quick checks:

- Mapping the game tree helps you see how choices explode and which paths truly matter.

- Reducing state space through symmetry and canonical forms makes deep analysis feasible.

- Understanding solvability in slices informs rule design and helps prevent hidden biases from shaping play.

Coming up next Subtittle: Publishing, Community, and Evolving Designs

1) Prototyping to production: art, components, and manufacturing constraints,

2) Building community: rulesets, variants, and tournament formats,

3) Iterative post-release support and evolving metagame

3. Using software to refine balance and discover emergent tactics

You're chasing balance and fresh tactics without trying to predict every move by hand. Software can help you run quick tests, spot surprising patterns, and reveal how players might bend the system in unintended ways. The goal is to learn what the game encourages at scale, then steer it toward richer, fairer play.

Step 1: Pick approachable tools. You don't need a laboratory full of gear. Start with accessible options like spreadsheet modeling for balance metrics, small scripts for automated play, or simple boardgame simulators that support custom rules. Rationale: ease of access lowers the barrier to experimentation and iteration.

Step 2: Define clear balance metrics. Decide on a few measurable targets: symmetry of starting options, consistency of outcome across variations, and the presence of meaningful decisions per turn. Rationale: concrete metrics keep experiments focused and comparable over time.

Step 3: Create automated tests. Build lightweight tests that adjust a single parameter at a time—like move value, capture cost, or territory weight—and run many trials to see how outcomes shift. Rationale: automated tests let you separate cause from effect and avoid random luck misguiding decisions.

Step 4: Run experiments to surface emergent tactics. Let the system explore many play-throughs with different rules and tweak variables to see if players start exploiting surprising patterns. Rationale: emergence is where real depth often hides, so you must look for it with broad testing.

Step 5: Record results methodically. Keep a simple log of parameter changes, outcomes, and any notable patterns. Rationale: you'll reuse this data when you refine or revert changes, and you'll build a history of what works.

Step 6: Apply informed adjustments and re-test. Make small, reversible changes to rules or balance, then run the same tests again to confirm that the shift moved the needle as intended. Rationale: iterative calibration keeps you moving toward a balanced, engaging system rather than chasing a moving target.

Example 1: You build a scoring system that rewards territory and penalizes stalling. With a handful of runs, you notice players start chasing long, slow paths that extend games beyond reasonable length. You tweak the scoring to reward decisive, shorter routes and re-run, which nudges plays toward quicker, sharper decisions without eliminating strategic depth.

Example 2: In a variant with resourceless play, you test a minor rule that generates a temporary advantage for early movers. The experiments show a slight first-move edge, but it's not overwhelming. You adjust to a softer early advantage and watch how tactics evolve—mid-game fights become crisper, and players look for multi-step plans rather than single-shot gambits.

Troubleshooting and quick fixes:

- If simulations drift toward any single tactic, scale back that tactic's weight and re-test to balance exploration and exploitation.

- If software feels slow or clumsy, simplify the model to a core core loop and gradually reintroduce complexity.

- If data is hard to interpret, visualize results with side-by-side comparisons across parameter sets to spot trends quickly.

- If emergent tactics look unhealthy or unfair, constrain them with guardrails that preserve strategic depth while avoiding exploitation.

Tools and templates you can use:

- A balance metric template: a simple table listing parameters, their target ranges, and observed outcomes.

- An experiment log: date, changes, metrics, observations, and next steps.

- A quick-start template for a minimalist rule set and its tests, ready to copy into a spreadsheet or small script.

Two micro-cases to show how software helps:

- Micro-case E: You test a small set of rule changes that affect timing and tempo. Automated tests show tempo shifts aren't just cosmetic—they change win rates in predictable ways. You narrow the changes to keep tempo lively but not chaotic.

- Micro-case F: You run a wide sweep of variations in a controlled sandbox to discover a previously unseen tactic that players can only access when several conditions align. You decide whether to constrain that tactic with a rule tweak or keep it as a high-skill option, then test again for balance.

Key takeaways and quick checks:

- Software helps you see patterns humans might miss in quick play sessions.

- Small, reversible changes and careful data logging keep experimentation safe and productive.

- Emergent tactics are a sign of depth, but they should be discoverable and controllable through thoughtful design.

Coming up next Subtittle: Publishing, Community, and Evolving Designs

1) Prototyping to production: art, components, and manufacturing constraints,

2) Building community: rulesets, variants, and tournament formats,

3) Iterative post-release support and evolving metagame

Key Takeaway: Use focused testing, state awareness, and lightweight software to balance your game, reveal useful tactics, and guide design choices toward deeper, fairer play. Coming up next Subtittle: Publishing, Community, and Evolving Designs

1) Prototyping to production: art, components, and manufacturing constraints,

2) Building community: rulesets, variants, and tournament formats,

3) Iterative post-release support and evolving metagame

Chapter 10

Publishing, Community, and Evolving Designs

By the end of this chapter, you will know how to move from prototype to production, build a community around your design, and plan ongoing updates that evolve the metagame.

Prototyping to production: art, components, and manufacturing constraints

You start with a simple idea and a cheap prototype. Your first goal is to test the core mechanic, the way players interact with pieces, and how easy the game is to learn. Keep the prototype plain and functional. Cardboard, paper, and basic tokens avoid distraction and let you focus on rules, not artwork. You'll learn fast what works and what doesn't by watching players pick up moves, read the board, and explain the rules back to you. This early stage is for clarity, not for polish.

As you test, you begin thinking about how the game could exist beyond a desk drawer. Manufacturing constraints matter sooner than you realize. A good rule is to choose materials and a board size that are easy to produce in multiple scales. Simple shapes, standard thicknesses, and clean edgework help keep costs predictable. If your pieces require unusual cuts or multiple colors, ask: could I achieve the same feel with fewer colors, fewer shapes, or a single tile style? When in doubt, prefer fewer moving parts and fewer tools for players to manage. Clear, robust tokens that are easy to grab, slide, and stack reduce fatigue and confusion during long sessions.

Two micro-cases illustrate the path from rough prototype to production decisions. Case one uses a grid-based board with a handful of wooden or cardboard tokens. Testers immediately grasp the intent because the pieces have distinct silhouettes and high-contrast colors. The learning curve stays friendly, and you notice that players automatically line up moves and plan ahead rather than rushing through turns. After several playtests, you decide to keep the shapes simple and switch to sturdier tokens. The result: faster setup, better readability, and a more confident group of testers who want to play again soon. Case two introduces modular tiles that players arrange to form different boards before each session. You discover that the modular approach increases replayability but also raises production complexity. To balance this, you scale back the number of unique modules and standardize connections so tiles snap cleanly and don't slip during play. The feel stays fresh, but production stays manageable and predictable.

A practical production path emerges when you write a simple production spec. You list the core components: board size, piece shapes, token counts, any dice or timers, and the basic packaging. You note color choices with accessibility in mind—colors that are easy to distinguish for players with common visual differences. You consider whether you'll publish a print-and-play version before committing to a full print run, or if you'll skip straight to small-batch production for a local audience. You plan for legibility in rule text and quick-reference summaries sewn into the board or onto sturdy player aids. And you reflect on assembly: can a beginner assemble the game with minimal tools in a few minutes? If yes, the prototype has earned a path toward production.

To keep you organized, use a Prototype-to-Production Checklist:

1. Define the core mechanic and every piece needed to support it.

2. Sketch board layout and piece shapes with manufacturability in mind.

3. Build a low-cost prototype using household materials and test with real players.

4. Run quick, focused playtests to measure readability, handling, and learning speed.

5. Note three concrete improvements for readability, handling, and rules clarity.

6. Decide on a production path (print-and-play, small batch, or mass market) based on budget and audience.

7. Create a simple production spec: sizes, quantities, materials, and color choices.

8. Produce a one-page rule summary and a quick-reference card to aid teaching.

9. Validate the design again with a fresh group before any formal order.

10. Plan an inexpensive pilot run to confirm tolerances in real-world manufacturing.

Two quick, practical tactics help you move efficiently. First, design for readability over complexity. If testers consistently ask "what does that tile do?" you simplify the symbol set or add a one-sentence reminder on the board. Second, test ergonomics as you test balance. If players strain to pick a piece or misread tiny icons, scale up tokens or simplify shapes so that handling becomes second nature. You don't want production constraints to sully the core fun of the game.

What you learn from production thinking at this stage is a gift: it makes your rules sharper and your game more robust in real life. You'll avoid last-minute scrambles when a printing vendor asks for exact tolerances or when you field questions about component weight, finish, or color range. Keep your notes concise and concrete. If something doesn't feel durable enough for repeated plays, consider a more robust material or a simpler design that can be replicated consistently. The aim is a clear, reliable experience, not a grand, fragile artifact.

Examples of how production thinking shapes design decisions. Example one: you start with a bright, glossy board and several colorful tokens. Players love the look, but during a demonstration you notice glare makes the board hard to read under bright lamp light. You switch to a matte finish and darker, high-contrast token colors. The change keeps the fun intact while improving long sessions without eye strain. Example two: you imagine fancy dice that double as teaching aids for demonstrating scoring. When you test, you realize players need to slow down to read the symbols. You replace the dice with flat chits that sit on the board more stably, keeping the pace brisk and the learning curve gentle. Small shifts like these keep the game accessible and resilient.

Tools and templates you can copy. A simple production spec template helps you stay consistent. Use a one-page sheet that lists: title, base mechanic, board dimensions, piece types and counts, token sizes, color palette, finishing options, packaging concept, and a quick rule summary. A separate “teach-and-play” sheet summarizes the turn sequence, victory conditions, and at-a-glance examples of key moves. Finally, keep a basic risk register: what could go wrong in manufacturing, how you'll test for it, and the simplest mitigation. These documents protect you from miscommunication and give your team a shared, easy-to-reference baseline.

Key takeaways from this section are simple to remember: design with production in mind from the first prototype, and simplify to keep costs predictable and playtested experiences consistent. If the prototype looks promising but tests reveal that production would be tricky or expensive, go back to the drawing board and strip the design to its essential heart. The game should feel both sturdy and approachable, no matter how small the initial run or how large the final audience.

Building community: rulesets, variants, and tournament formats

A game becomes a living thing when players feel invited to modify it, remix it, and test new ideas without breaking the core rules. You invite collaboration by offering clear, accessible rulesets and lightweight variants that add optional twists rather than overhaul the entire system. The base game stays the same, but players can opt into clever add-ons that keep play fresh. When you publish variants, you help players understand how to teach them, what to watch for, and how to balance new ideas with the original design.

Two concrete micro-cases show how variants and formats can grow a community. Case one introduces a simple rules variant called a "zone twist." In this variant, certain zones on the board have special, limited actions. The rules are written in plain language, with quick-start examples so players can try it in their first game. After playing with the variant in three sessions, you collect feedback on understanding, balance, and fun. The results help you decide whether to fold the variant into the core rulebook, keep it as a separate downloadable option, or retire it if it causes confusion. Case two explores a lightweight tournament format. You pilot a small Swiss-style event with four players, two rounds, and clear pairings. You publish a short guide that explains the format, how ties are resolved, and how to report scores. The format makes it easier for players to join and for organizers to run events, which in turn grows your community.

A practical approach to community building runs on three pillars: clarity, openness, and consistency. First, publish a clean ruleset with a concise teaching flow. Players should be able to explain the game to a new person in two minutes or less. Second, publish one or two variants that are easy to explain, clearly separated from the base rules, and tested to ensure they don't cheapen or overpower the core experience. Third, publish a simple tournament framework that players can replicate in local stores, clubs, or school rooms. A predictable path to play and compete builds enthusiasm, trust, and a sense of belonging.

You'll also want to establish a lightweight governance plan. Decide how to handle disputes, how to incorporate player feedback, and how to publish official updates without erasing prior versions for new players. Maintain a version log and a prominent disclaimer that variants are optional and that the base rules remain the foundation. This approach preserves the integrity of the original design while encouraging experimentation and community growth.

A practical variant and tournament toolkit helps you stay organized. Variant Template: Name, Purpose, Added Rules, Teaching Notes, Balancing Considerations, and Retirement Criteria. Tournament Format Template: Name, Player Count, Rounds, Pairing Method, Tie-Break Rules, and How to Record Results. You can share these in your game's instruction sheet or as a downloadable PDF, so players can quickly set up an event and play.

Three short exercises to cultivate community-building momentum. Exercise 1: Run a 30-minute playtest session with a new variant and capture questions players have about the added rules. Time the session, record responses, and note which rules need a one-page teaching aid. Exercise 2: Draft one lightweight variant and test it with two different groups in two separate sessions. Compare clarity and balance across groups and write a one-paragraph summary of each group's experience. Exercise 3: Organize a mini-tournament with four players using the base rules and one agreed-upon variant. Track time to teach, number of turns per game, and the ease of resolving ties. Use the data to decide whether to publish the variant or refine it further.

Common pitfalls and quick fixes in building community. If players misinterpret a variant, fix by adding a near-perfect teaching example and a one-page quick-start. If a tournament feels chaotic, tighten the rules for pairings and tie-breaks, and publish a simple score sheet with clear fields. If the base rules are hard to learn, improve the human-friendly teaching flow: add a two-minute explained playthrough at the start of every session and provide a one-page glossary of key terms. Shaping a healthy community takes steady, small adjustments rather than dramatic overhauls. Keep communications welcoming and inclusive, document decisions, and celebrate small wins with your players.

Iterative post-release support and evolving metagame

A game's life continues after release. Players discover new tactics, combinations, and strategies that you hadn't anticipated. The metagame—how players use the rules to win—starts to emerge. Your job is to observe, learn, and respond in a way that preserves balance and fun while keeping the door open for fresh ideas. Gather feedback from playgroups, clubs, and online discussions. Look for patterns: what moves become common, which setups feel sluggish, which variants spark the most excitement. Use that information to plan small, safe updates rather than sweeping changes.

Two micro-cases show how careful post-release work pays off. Case one watches a group of players gradually favor a particular approach and notes that the base rules still allow it but the tempo shifts in that direction. You adjust the recommended tutorial emphasis and publish a simple counterexample that teaches players how to recognize and counterbalance the trend. The result is a healthier spread of tactics and a more teachable path for new players. Case two identifies a confusing edge case that early players stumble over during the first few games. You release a clear FAQ with a couple of concrete examples and add a one-page "how-to-teach-this-rule" sheet to aid future sessions. Players respond with increased confidence and speed, and new players arrive with fewer questions.

A disciplined update process helps you manage the evolving metagame. Maintain a change log that records what was changed, why it was changed, and how players can adapt. Communicate changes with a short, practical explanation and provide examples of how the new rule behaves in typical situations. Keep backward compatibility in mind whenever possible, so players who prefer older versions aren't left behind. When you do make a larger update, consider running a brief, time-limited pilot in communities that express interest, and publish results along with guidance on when and how to adopt the new version. The aim is steady improvement that honors players' time and imagination.

Examples of metagame evolution help you anticipate what to expect. Example one shows a community experimenting with a new endgame condition that shifts the balance late in the game. You test this condition in a handful of sessions and observe how players adjust their midgame plans. After balancing tweaks and a couple of clarifying notes, the new condition becomes a recognized element of the metagame, enriching decisions rather than complicating them. Example two demonstrates how a quiet FAQ can reduce friction. A single, well-placed clarification eliminates several recurring questions, allowing new players to join with less hesitation and enabling longer, more satisfying sessions.

A practical post-release toolkit helps you stay ahead. Change Log Template: Version Number, Date, What Changed, Why, Teaching Notes, and Migration Guidance. Player Feedback Sheet: Question prompts, a simple 1–5 rating, and space for open notes. Release Play Guide: a short script for teaching new rules to groups, including corner cases and suggested pacing. You can reuse these tools as you grow your library of variants and your community.

Key takeaways from this section are straightforward. Publish clear, optional variants that invite experimentation without breaking the base experience. Build a simple, welcoming tournament structure that is easy to replicate locally. Finally, run small, careful post-release updates that address real problems, collect feedback, and keep the game balanced and engaging over time.

Transition: In the next chapter, you'll explore the history and inspirations behind abstract game design, seeing how classic games and early ideas shaped these practical approaches. You'll learn why these principles matter and how they connect to timeless strategies that players around the world have enjoyed for generations. This historical awareness will deepen your intuition as you prototype, build communities, and guide ongoing evolution of your own designs.

Dear Reader,

Thank you for exploring this series focused on failures and the power of comeback stories. If you find value in these stories and believe in the importance of embracing setbacks as part of growth, we appreciate your support. Please consider sharing a positive review on the platform where you accessed this series.

Your feedback helps spread the message, inspiring more young readers to see challenges as opportunities and to believe in their potential. We understand that mistakes happen, and we thank you for your understanding.

www.ingramcontent.com/pod-product-compliance
Lightning Source LLC
LaVergne TN
LVHW052321200926
848481LV00002B/629
9798295508226